Living with Climate Change

Quiz No 217007
Living with Climate Change

Sage, Alison
B.L.: 4.9
Points: 0.5   LY

Contents

D1355030

Collins   Written by Alison Sage

Our climate is changing

All around the world, the climate is different. Some places are cool and wet. Some are boiling hot and dry. But wherever we are, we know the kind of weather to expect. Or at least, we used to.

Today, we know that everywhere, the climate is changing. The problem is, we don't know exactly how much, or when. We don't even know for sure *what* will happen *where*.

Weather facts

Climate is the kind of weather you can expect throughout the year. At the **North Pole** it's freezing, but at the **equator** it's much hotter.

Weather is what happens from day to day: rain, sun, wind or snow.

Global warming

Today, the world is warmer than it's been for a thousand years. But **global** warming doesn't only mean that our weather is getting hotter. It means that it's getting harder to **predict**. Some places are dry, when they should be wet, some places have huge storms and a year's rainfall in a few days.

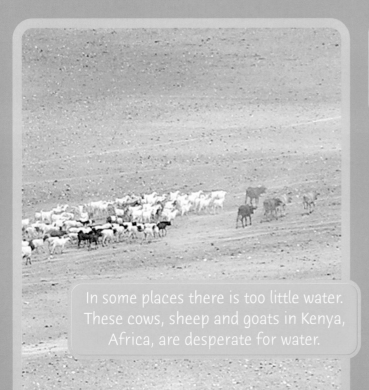

In some places there is too little water. These cows, sheep and goats in Kenya, Africa, are desperate for water.

In other places, like Bihar, India, they have too much water, too quickly. Many people drowned here when floodwater rose higher than 2 metres.

The greenhouse effect

The world is warming up a little more every year and the warmer it gets, the more **unpredictable** the weather will be. So, why's this happening?

Scientists think they know why. When we burn fuel – like oil or coal or wood – we make a gas called **carbon dioxide** (**CO_2**). Today, there is more CO_2 in the air than there has been for more than half a million years. Together with other gases, carbon dioxide acts like a greenhouse, trapping the heat from the Sun's rays. Think of what would happen if you sat outside on a sunny day in a plastic mac. You'd get hotter and hotter.

Carbon dioxide in the air acts like a greenhouse.

Trees use up carbon dioxide in the air. If we cut down forests, we have fewer trees to help control carbon dioxide. Also, cities are growing and there are more and more cars and factories, which all pump out carbon dioxide into the air. So the problem of too much carbon dioxide in the air gets worse.

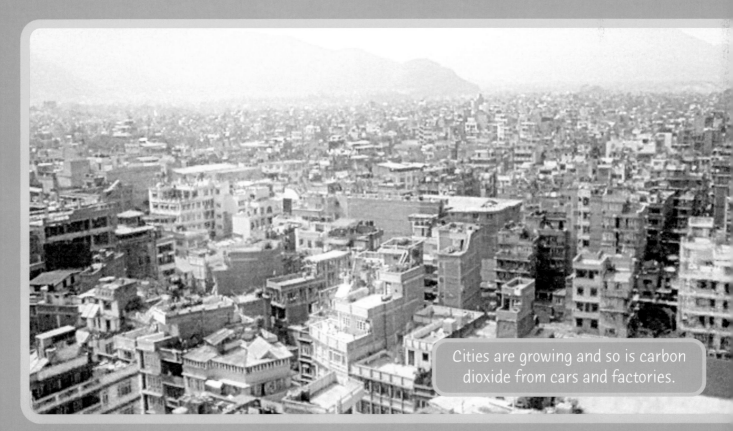

Cities are growing and so is carbon dioxide from cars and factories.

Melting ice

The seas are warming up too and the massive **ice sheets** at the North Pole and **South Pole** have started to melt. If the ice sheets melt, this will unlock a huge amount of water. **Sea levels** all around the world will rise and this means that there will be more floods.

Huge ice sheets are melting at the North and South Poles.

"Natural" disasters

Very hot weather with no rain, storms and floods all cause disasters. In many countries, children suffer most in these "natural" disasters. But these children are learning to live with climate change and thinking about ways to get ready for the future.

Pascal from Guatemala is planting a tree.

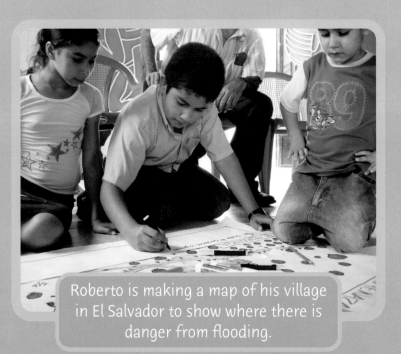

Roberto is making a map of his village in El Salvador to show where there is danger from flooding.

Bangladesh, Asia

Bangladesh is a hot and **fertile** country. It's also very wet. For nine months
of the year it can rain very heavily and its great rivers flood every year,
watering the fields and covering them with fertile mud. But today, the floods are
more violent and harder to predict. They're especially dangerous for Bangladeshis
who live in the rivers on sandy islands called chars. Floods wash away their
homes and sometimes the islands themselves vanish under water.

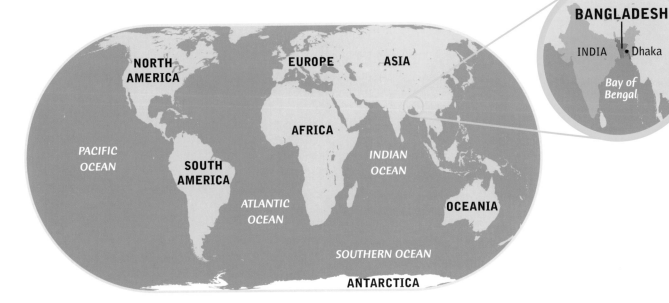

NORTH
AMERICA

EUROPE

ASIA

AFRICA

PACIFIC
OCEAN

SOUTH
AMERICA

INDIAN
OCEAN

ATLANTIC
OCEAN

OCEANIA

SOUTHERN OCEAN

ANTARCTICA

BANGLADESH

INDIA • Dhaka

Bay of
Bengal

These children from Shindurna char, Bangladesh, are going to school through the floods.

average rainfall in July in northern Bangladesh: 60 cm

average rainfall in July in London, England: 5 cm

9

I'm Shumi and I live in Bangladesh. When the floods came last year I picked up my little brother and ran to the road, which is on high ground. The water crept up higher and higher until it reached my knees. I was so scared, but my dad came and carried us into the house. We climbed up to the roof and stayed there for five days. There was no fresh water to drink and afterwards I had a bad fever.

When I get older I'll tie ropes along the roads, so that people can see them even in a flood and they won't drown.

Shumi and her little brother outside their house

The roads are higher than the fields, so we can move about easily. But in the floods, water covers the roads, and we can't find our way.

Shumi at school

I'm Mainul and I live in Bangladesh. Last year, the floods came with no warning and the water in our house reached as high as my dad's chest. Everything was spoilt, my schoolbooks, clothes, our rice – everything. We lifted up our beds with rope and my mother made our food on her bed. We lived like this for nearly a week and all our chickens and our cow were washed away and drowned. My grandmother says that these floods are much worse than the ones when she was my age.

When I get older I'll build my house on high ground, on a platform, so that the water doesn't pour in. My friend Shahidul says that the radio could tell everyone when the bad floods are coming. Then we could get ready for them.

Mainul doing his homework

Shahidul and his family's radio

Mainul looking after his family's cow

Kenya, Africa

Kenya is a beautiful country on the equator and although some parts are very hot and wet, much of it is very dry. It only rains at certain times of the year and people depend on "the rains" for drinking water and to grow their food. But the rains are becoming less and less reliable. Sometimes they don't come at all and when this happens **crops** die and families have little food to eat.

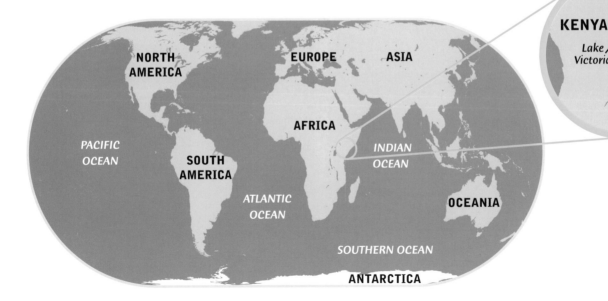

Many children have their one meal of the day at school.

When no rain falls, the crops die and there's no food. Some children have to eat berries because they're hungry.

I'm Munene. There used to be many wild animals where we live and I liked collecting honey from the bees' nests in the trees, but now there's nothing because people have cut the trees down. After school, I look after our goats, but I have to go far to find water and grass for them and many have died. When I grow up I'll plant more trees.

This is Munene.

This is Munene's friend Peter collecting water. The cattle and goats are very thin.

14

I'm Kathure. I don't understand climate change, but I know that the rivers have dried up and I have to walk a long way to collect water. I only have one meal a day, which I'm given at school. I feel so bad when I see my baby brother crying because he's hungry and I can't do anything. I wish I could change this.

When I grow up, I'll plant crops that don't need much rain to grow. Then my family will have food.

Joy is Kathure's cousin. She's grinding millet to make flour. Millet doesn't need so much water to grow.

Kathure and her mother and granny and little brother. Kathure walks 5 kilometres to collect water before she goes to school.

Haiti, Caribbean

Haiti is part of the island of Hispaniola in the Caribbean. Between August and October is the hurricane season, but nowadays these dangerous storms seem to happen more often. Scientists think this is because of global warming. Hurricanes begin over the sea and when they strike land, they flatten everything in their path, bringing floods, smashing homes and ripping up crops.

HISPANIOLA
Cuba
Dominican Republic
Port-au-Prince
HAITI
Caribbean Sea

NORTH AMERICA
EUROPE
ASIA
AFRICA
SOUTH AMERICA
PACIFIC OCEAN
ATLANTIC OCEAN
INDIAN OCEAN
OCEANIA
SOUTHERN OCEAN
ANTARCTICA

A hurricane is a huge tropical storm. It's hundreds of kilometres wide and spins round in a circle. In the middle, the "eye" of the storm is calm. Hurricanes are given names like Katrina, Ike or Noel. Hurricanes need warm sea water to develop and grow. They do terrible damage when they reach land, but at that point, they begin to get weaker and fade away.

a hurricane

warm sea

wall of cloud and storm developing

eye

The spinning wall of cloud and storm is where the wind speed is highest and rainfall heaviest.

Weather facts

Hurricanes can bring:

- **winds of over 200 kilometres per hour**
- **gigantic storm waves of more than 7 metres high**
- **more than 50 centimetres of rain in 24 hours.**

This is Jude.

flooding in Jacmel, Haiti, after Hurricane Ike

My name is Jude and I live on the coast in Haiti. One night, Hurricane Ike came. Dad had boarded up the house, but he's a policeman and was at work. Outside, the road turned into a river rushing past. It was full of all kinds of stuff – dead chickens and goats and lumps of wood smashing into everything. Then it went dark. The power was off and water was pouring into the house. Mum grabbed me and my little brother and held us tight. I was very scared. Scared to die, scared that the water would take away my family and my friends. I was also afraid to lose my house because we don't have enough money to build another.

Our house survived, but in the morning I saw my friend's roof was torn off, power lines were ripped up and buildings were smashed. Many people died that night.

When I grow up, I'll make houses that don't break up when hurricanes come.

In 2007, Hurricane Felix missed Haiti but it hit Nicaragua. Hundreds of people were killed and thousands lost their homes overnight.

The Philippines, Asia

The Philippines are a group of islands in the Pacific Ocean. They have high mountains and great natural beauty, but they also have some of the worst typhoons in the world. Today, they get about 21 typhoons a year and scientists think that global warming could be making these storms worse.

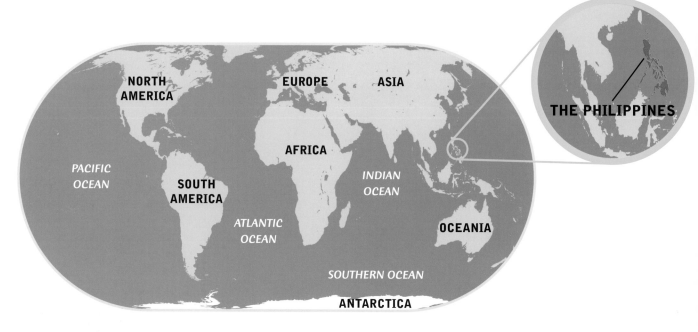

THE PHILIPPINES

NORTH AMERICA

EUROPE

ASIA

AFRICA

PACIFIC OCEAN

SOUTH AMERICA

INDIAN OCEAN

ATLANTIC OCEAN

OCEANIA

SOUTHERN OCEAN

ANTARCTICA

Typhoons, bringing heavy rain and wind, cause mudslides. If trees have been cut down, there is nothing to stop the mud pouring down the mountainside on to the villages beneath.

mud

cut-down trees

village

Mudslides are very dangerous because they travel much faster than anyone can run and can bury a village in soft, sinking mud in minutes.

After a storm, wet earth and mud slides down the steep slopes where there are no trees.

This is Marissa.

Marissa and her friends are planting trees and plants to stop mudslides.

I'm Marissa and I'll never forget the day of the mudslide. At about ten in the morning, I heard a strange roaring sound and looked outside. The top of the mountain was crumbling, falling. I was so afraid. In the next village, the school and all the children were buried under tons and tons of wet mud and rocks. My auntie tried to dig for my two cousins with her bare hands, but she couldn't find them.

Afterwards, we children knew that our school could be buried too. We got everyone to rebuild it in a safer place. We've started planting trees, and checking to see how much it's rained. If there's a lot of rain in a short time, then we can tell when the mudslides are coming.

When I grow up, I'll make sure that people know when they're in danger.

Marissa looks out over some of the land where the mudslide came.

These things all burn fuel and make carbon dioxide, leaving a carbon footprint.

If you walk on the sand, you leave a footprint. Burning fuel makes carbon dioxide and so we say it leaves a **carbon footprint**. Whenever you go in a car, or a plane, or use electricity or gas, you're burning fuel and so you're leaving a carbon footprint.

London, England

We're Callum and Nina and we live in London. We're trying to make our carbon footprint smaller by walking to school. We've also started **recycling** as much as we can. The more we stop throwing things away, the less fuel gets used up making new things. And we're trying to grow our own vegetables, so that our food doesn't have to travel so far.

We're also planting trees. Every new tree helps to fight global warming because trees use up carbon dioxide.

Sam is planting a tree in his school garden.

Callum and Nina are working in their school garden.

What can we do?

The world has a long history and there have been many changes to the climate since our planet began. But every big change makes big problems for the animals living at the time – and that includes humans. Climate change means that some animals like polar bears, some kinds of insects, birds and even plants are in danger of dying out because their environment is changing.

These creatures are in danger because of climate change.

We probably can't stop global warming altogether, but we can learn how to live with it and slow it down. We can't stop using fuel, but we can use it more carefully. In that way, climate change won't mean global disaster and our world will be a good place to live.

Lily and her little sister Petra are planting a tree with their teacher in Scotland.

Bao from Thailand is looking after a young tree.

carbon dioxide	a gas that is produced by burning fuels
carbon footprint	the carbon dioxide we create and leave behind by burning fuel
CO₂	the chemical formula for carbon dioxide
crops	the amount of food that is grown at one time
equator	an imaginary line drawn around the centre of the Earth at equal distances from the North and South Poles
fertile	capable of growing things
global	something that is to do with the whole world
ice sheets	layers of ice that cover large areas of land for a long period of time
North Pole	the point furthest north on the Earth
predict	to try to work out what will happen in the future, based on what is known at the moment
recycling	converting waste products into reusable material
sea levels	the height of the sea's surface
South Pole	the point furthest south on the Earth
unpredictable	an event that people did not think would happen

Index

To reduce our carbon footprint:

• recycle

• plant more trees

• walk, cycle or take the bus

• grow your own vegetables

How can children get ready for climate change?

Floods:

• have fresh water and food in the house

• build houses on high ground

• listen out for storm warnings on the radio

• tie ropes along the roads so they can be easily seen

Hurricanes:

- have fresh water and food in the house
- in the future build strong houses in safe places

Drought:

- plant more trees
- learn what crops grow best with little water

Mudslides:

- check that houses and schools are built in safe places
- monitor the rainfall as that causes mudslides
- warn people when mudslides are coming
- plant trees

Ideas for guided reading

Learning objectives: identify and make notes of the main points of sections of texts; identify how different texts are organised; explain process or present information, ensuring items are clearly sequenced, relevant details are included and accounts are ended effectively

Curriculum links: Geography: Passport to the world, Weather around the world; Science: Characteristics of materials

Interest words: climate, carbon dioxide, carbon footprint, drought, equator, global, hurricane, ice sheets, recycling, typhoon, unpredictable

Resources: ICT, world map, resource sheet for note-making

Getting started

This book can be read over two or more guided reading sessions.

- Ask children to describe the weather outside. Introduce the word *climate* and discuss what it means in relation to children's experience of weather.

- Look at the front and back covers of *Living with Climate Change*. Read the blurb. Discuss what *Climate Change* might mean and how it may affect the children's lives.

- Read through the contents together. Ask children to find the names of the countries included: *Bangladesh, Kenya, Haiti, The Philippines, England.* Show children where the countries are on a world map and ask them to predict the climate in each place.

Reading and responding

- Read pp2–3 with the children. Ask children to notice how the text is organised. What features does the author use? *fact boxes, photographs, captions, bold type.*

- In pairs, ask children to read pp4–7, making a note of some key points. Remind children to use the glossary and photographs to help them make meaning.

- Ask children to share the key points from their reading. Check that they understand that weather is becoming more unpredictable due to the greenhouse effect.